contents

haricot bean soup

2 cups (400g) dried haricot beans
1 tablespoon olive oil
2 medium onions, chopped finely
1 clove garlic, crushed
2 large carrots, chopped finely
2 trimmed celery stalks, chopped finely
1.5kg tomatoes, peeled, deseeded, chopped
2 vegetable stock cubes
⅓ cup (80ml) tomato paste
2.5 litres (10 cups) hot water
¼ cup chopped fresh flat-leaf parsley

1 Place beans in bowl, cover well with water; cover, stand overnight. Drain beans, rinse well.
2 Heat oil in saucepan, add onions and garlic; cook, stirring, until soft. Add carrots and celery, cook over low heat, stirring mixture occasionally, 10 minutes. Stir in tomatoes, crumbled stock cubes and paste.
3 Add beans and hot water; simmer, covered, 1½ hours or until beans are tender. Stir in two-thirds of the parsley; season with salt and pepper to taste.
4 Divide soup among serving bowls; serve, sprinkled with remaining parsley.

serves 8 to 10

chicken soup with egg & lemon

1.4kg chicken
4 litres (16 cups) water
2 black peppercorns
1 medium carrot, chopped
1 medium onion, chopped
1 celery stalk, chopped
½ cup (100g) short-grain rice
2 eggs
¼ cup (60ml) lemon juice

1 Combine chicken, water, peppercorns, carrot, onion and celery in large saucepan; simmer, covered, 2 hours.

2 Remove chicken from pan, reserve for another use. Strain stock through sieve; discard vegetables. Cool stock; cover, refrigerate overnight. Skim fat from stock. You will need around 2.25 litres (9 cups) stock.

3 Bring stock to boil in saucepan; add rice, cook, partly covered, 15 minutes or until rice is tender, stirring occasionally. Season with salt and pepper to taste.

4 Just before serving, whisk eggs and juice in medium bowl until frothy. Gradually whisk in 2 cups (500ml) of hot stock. Whisk egg and lemon mixture into pan of remaining hot stock and rice mixture; whisk over heat until heated through. Do not boil.

serves 6 to 8

seafood soup

300g medium uncooked prawns
1 small lobster tail (about 200g)
1.2kg fish heads and bones
1 large onion, chopped
1 trimmed celery stalk, chopped
1 medium carrot, chopped
2 bay leaves
8 sprigs fresh lemon thyme
2 litres (8 cups) water
2 tablespoons olive oil
1 large leek, sliced
3 cloves garlic, thinly sliced
1 trimmed celery stalk, chopped, extra
3 medium tomatoes, peeled, deseeded, chopped
1½ tablespoons chopped fresh lemon thyme
½ cup (125ml) dry white wine
¼ cup (60ml) tomato paste
½ teaspoon fennel seeds
1 large potato, chopped
1 teaspoon sugar
250g firm white fish fillets
150g scallops
2 tablespoons chopped fresh parsley
¼ cup (60ml) lemon juice

1 Shell and devein prawns, discard heads, reserve shells. Remove lobster meat from shell, reserve shell. Reserve prawn and lobster meat for soup. Combine reserved prawn and lobster shells, fish heads and bones, onion, celery, carrot, bay leaves, lemon thyme sprigs and water in saucepan; simmer, uncovered, 35 minutes. Strain stock, discard fish heads and bones and vegetables. You will need 1.5 litres (6 cups) stock.

2 Heat oil in saucepan, add leek and garlic; cook, stirring, until leek is soft. Add extra celery, tomatoes, chopped lemon thyme and wine; boil, uncovered, until vegetables are soft.

3 Stir in combined stock, paste and seeds; simmer, uncovered, 10 minutes. Add potato, simmer 5 minutes or until potato is just tender. Add sugar; season with salt and pepper to taste.

4 Cut reserved lobster meat and fish into 4cm pieces. Add fish pieces to soup, simmer 1 minute; add lobster and reserved prawns, simmer further minute. Add scallops, bring to boil, stir in parsley and juice.

serves 6

prawns with feta

24 large uncooked prawns (about 1.4kg)
2 tablespoons olive oil
4 spring onions, chopped
2 teaspoons grated lemon rind
1 teaspoon lemon pepper
1 tablespoon chopped fresh oregano
1 tablespoon chopped fresh parsley
1 tablespoon chopped fresh thyme
2 medium tomatoes, peeled, deseeded, chopped
200g feta cheese, crumbled
tomato sauce
30g butter
1 medium onion, chopped finely
4 cloves garlic, crushed
425g can tomatoes
2 tablespoons tomato paste
⅓ cup (80ml) dry white wine
½ cup (125ml) chicken stock
½ teaspoon sugar

1 Make tomato sauce.
2 Shell prawns, leaving tails intact. Remove dark vein using sharp knife.
3 Heat oil in large frying pan, add prawns, onions, rind and lemon pepper; cook, stirring, until prawns change colour.
4 Stir in the tomato sauce, herbs and tomatoes; stir over heat until heated through. Serve sprinkled with cheese.

tomato sauce Heat butter in saucepan, add onion and garlic; cook, stirring, until onion is soft. Add undrained crushed tomatoes and remaining ingredients; stir until boiling. Blend or process sauce until smooth; strain.

serves 6

courgette fritters with yogurt dip

5 large courgettes (750g), grated
1 medium onion, chopped finely
1½ cup (75g) plain flour
3 eggs, beaten lightly
1 tablespoon chopped fresh
  oregano
1 tablespoon chopped fresh basil
1 tablespoon chopped fresh parsley
oil for shallow-frying
yogurt dip
¼ cup (180ml) plain greek yogurt
1 small cucumber, deseeded, grated
1 clove garlic, crushed
1 tablespoon chopped fresh mint
2 teaspoons lemon juice

1 Combine courgettes, onion, flour, eggs and herbs in bowl; season to taste with salt and pepper.
2 Shallow-fry level ¼ cups (60ml) of mixture in hot oil until lightly browned underneath; flatten slightly. Turn fritters, cook until well browned on other side and cooked through; drain on absorbent kitchen paper.
3 Meanwhile, combine all yogurt dip ingredients in bowl; mix well. Serve fritters with yogurt dip.

makes about 15

preserved lemons

6 medium unwaxed lemons (850g)
¼ cup (55g) coarse cooking salt
1 cup (250ml) lemon juice, approximately
1 cup (250ml) lime juice

1 Quarter lemons lengthways to within 5mm of the base.
2 Open out lemons, sprinkle cut surfaces with salt; reshape lemons.
3 Pack lemons very firmly into sterilized jar (1.5 litres/6 cup capacity), pour over enough combined juices to fill jar completely; seal jar.

to serve remove and discard pulp from rind. Squeeze juice from rind, rinse rind well; slice thinly. Serve as part of a platter with olives, cubed feta cheese and sprinkled with olive oil. Rind can also be used in casseroles, with fish and in salads, etc.

tip You will need the juice from approximately 4 lemons and 7 limes for this recipe.

tomato, leek & marinated feta tartlets

1 medium leek (350g)
20g butter
1 tablespoon olive oil
2 sheets ready-rolled puff pastry
250g cherry tomatoes, sliced thinly
½ teaspoon fresh thyme leaves
1 tablespoon red wine vinegar

marinated fetta
1 teaspoon finely grated lemon rind
¼ teaspoon cracked black pepper
2 cloves garlic, crushed
2 teaspoons fresh thyme leaves
200g feta cheese, cut into 24 pieces
1¼ cups (310ml) olive oil

1 Make marinated feta.

2 Preheat oven to hot.

3 Cut leek into 6cm pieces; cut pieces in half lengthways, slice halves lengthways into thin strips. Heat butter and oil in large frying pan; cook leek, stirring occasionally, about 20 minutes or until soft.

4 Meanwhile, cut each pastry sheet into twelve 6cm x 8cm rectangles; place on lightly oiled baking trays. Fold in each side to form a 2mm border; prick pastry pieces with fork. Bake, uncovered, in hot oven about 10 minutes or until browned lightly. Remove from oven; using fork, immediately press pastry pieces down to flatten. Reduce oven temperature to moderately hot.

5 Meanwhile, place tomato in medium bowl with thyme and vinegar; toss gently to combine.

6 Spread 1 tablespoon of the leek mixture over each pastry piece; crumble one piece of cheese over each then top with tomato mixture. Bake in moderately hot oven about 5 minutes or until tomato just softens. Serve immediately.

marinated feta Combine rind, pepper, garlic and thyme in medium sterilised glass jar having a tight-fitting lid; add cheese. Seal jar then shake gently to coat cheese in mixture. Open jar and pour in enough of the oil to completely cover cheese mixture. Reseal; refrigerate overnight.

makes 24

tips The feta can be marinated up to two weeks before making the tartlets; keep, covered, under refrigeration. Work with one puff pastry sheet at a time, keeping the other in the freezer so that it doesn't become too soft.

vine leaves with pine nuts & currants

300g packet vine leaves in brine
1 tablespoon lemon juice
¾ cup (180ml) water
1 tablespoon olive oil
filling
¼ cup (60ml) olive oil
1 medium onion, chopped finely
2 tablespoons pine nuts
½ cup (100g) short-grain rice
2 tablespoons currants
½ cup (125ml) water
2 tablespoons chopped fresh parsley

1 Make filling.
2 Rinse leaves under cold water; drain well. Place leaves vein side up on bench, place 2 level teaspoons of filling on each leaf; roll firmly, folding in sides, to enclose filling.
3 Place rolls in single layer over base of large heavy-based saucepan; add combined juice, water and oil. Place a plate on top of rolls to keep rolls in position during cooking. Simmer, covered, over low heat 1 hour.

filling Heat oil in saucepan, add onion; cook, stirring, until soft. Add nuts; cook, stirring, until lightly browned. Stir in rice and currants, mix well to coat rice in oil. Add water; simmer, covered, over low heat 10 minutes or until liquid is absorbed. Remove pan from heat; cool. Stir in parsley.

makes about 24
tip Vine leaves are available from delicatessens and supermarkets.

fig & feta bites

125g marinated feta cheese
1 tablespoon finely chopped fresh chives
24 melba toasts
3 medium fresh figs (180g)

1 Using fork, mash cheese with chives in small bowl; spread on
one side of each toast.
2 Cut each fig into eight wedges; place one wedge on each
toast. Sprinkle with coarsely ground black pepper, if desired.

makes 24
tip You can either purchase marinated feta at your favourite
delicatessen or make your own (see our recipe on page 12).

vine leaf cheese parcels

2 tablespoons finely chopped fresh basil
1 fresh small red thai chilli, chopped finely
2 teaspoons finely grated lemon rind
1 tablespoon lemon juice
2 teaspoons olive oil
500g graviera cheese, cut into 24 pieces (use gruyere if not available)
8 slices prosciutto (120g)
24 vine leaves in brine, rinsed, drained

1 Place basil, chilli, rind, juice and oil in bowl with cheese; toss gently to combine. Cut each prosciutto slice lengthways into three even strips.
2 Centre one cheese piece on each vine leaf; fold leaf over cheese to enclose completely. Wrap one strip of prosciutto around each vine-leaf parcel.
3 Heat large non-stick frying pan; cook parcels, uncovered, about 5 minutes or until prosciutto is crisp all over.

makes 24

mushroom filo triangles

60g butter
1 large onion, chopped
750g flat mushrooms, chopped
¼ cup (20g) grated parmesan cheese
⅓ cup (25g) stale breadcrumbs
14 sheets filo pastry
100g butter, melted, extra

1 Heat butter in saucepan; cook onion, stirring, until soft. Add mushrooms; cook, stirring, until mushrooms are tender and liquid evaporated. Remove from heat, stir in cheese and breadcrumbs; season to taste with salt and pepper.
2 Preheat oven to moderately hot. Lightly grease oven trays.
3 To prevent pastry from drying out, cover with baking parchment then a damp tea towel until you are ready to use it. Layer two sheets of pastry together, brushing each with a little extra butter. Cut layered sheets into four strips lengthways. Place 1 tablespoon of mushroom mixture at one end of each strip of pastry.
4 Fold one corner end of pastry diagonally across filling to other edge to form a triangle. Continue folding to end of strip, retaining triangular shape. Brush triangles with a little more extra butter. Repeat with remaining pastry, filling and extra butter. Place triangles on prepared trays. Bake in moderately hot oven 15 minutes or until browned.

makes 28

broad beans with peas & artichokes

3½ cups (500g) frozen broad beans, thawed
2 tablespoons olive oil
1 large onion, chopped finely
4 cloves garlic, crushed
2 medium carrots, chopped
2¼ cups (350g) shelled peas
425g can tomatoes
20 drained artichoke hearts, quartered
2 tablespoons chopped fresh dill

1 Add broad beans to saucepan of boiling water, boil 1 minute; drain, rinse under cold water until cold, drain well. Peel and discard outer skins.
2 Heat oil in saucepan, add onion, garlic and carrots; cook, stirring, until onion is soft. Stir in peas and undrained crushed tomatoes. Simmer, covered, 10 minutes or until peas are tender.
3 Add beans, artichokes and dill; stir over heat until heated through. Season with salt and pepper to taste.

serves 4 to 6
tip You need 1kg fresh peas for this recipe.

roasted vegetable & goats' cheese terrine

2 large red peppers (700g)
2 large aubergines (1kg), sliced thinly lengthways
2 medium courgettes (240g), sliced thinly lengthways
150g soft goats' cheese
¼ cup (60ml) double cream
1 tablespoon lemon juice
½ cup loosely packed fresh basil leaves
100g mixed salad leaves
basil oil
½ cup (125ml) extra virgin olive oil
½ cup loosely packed fresh basil leaves
10g baby spinach leaves
1 tablespoon finely grated lemon rind

1 Line 1.5-litre (6-cup) terrine dish with cling film.
2 Quarter peppers; discard seeds and membranes. Roast under grill or in very hot oven, skin-side up, until skin blisters and blackens. Cover pepper pieces in plastic or paper 5 minutes; peel away skin.
3 Cook aubergines and courgettes in lightly oiled large frying pan, in batches, until browned both sides.
4 Combine cheese, cream and juice in small bowl.
5 Line base and sides of prepared dish with two-thirds of the aubergine, draping it over all sides of dish. Place half of the pepper over base of dish; spread cheese mixture over pepper then top with basil, courgette, remaining pepper and remaining aubergine. Fold overhanging aubergine at short sides over terrine then fold remaining aubergines over long sides to completely enclose terrine. Cover; refrigerate 30 minutes.
6 Meanwhile, make basil oil.
7 Cut terrine into eight slices. Serve on salad leaves, drizzle with basil oil.

basil oil Blend or process ingredients until smooth. Strain through small muslin-lined strainer into small jug.

serves 8

greek salad

250g feta cheese
5 medium tomatoes
2 small cucumbers
1 large red onion, sliced
1 cup (160g) black olives
dressing
½ cup (125ml) olive oil
¼ cup (60ml) white vinegar
1 clove garlic, crushed
1 teaspoon sugar
1 teaspoon chopped fresh oregano

1 Combine all dressing ingredients in bowl; mix well.
2 Cut cheese into small cubes, cut tomatoes into wedges, cut cucumber into slices.
3 Combine cheese, tomatoes, onion, cucumbers and olives in bowl; drizzle with dressing.

serves 6

roasted tomatoes with crispy basil

500g baby vine tomatoes
2 cloves garlic, sliced thinly
1 tablespoon olive oil
2 teaspoons balsamic vinegar
vegetable oil, for deep-frying
⅓ cup loosely packed fresh basil
   leaves

1 Preheat oven to moderate.
2 Place tomatoes on baking tray. Combine garlic, oil and vinegar and pour over tomatoes. Roast, uncovered, in moderate oven about 10 minutes or until tomatoes soften.
3 Meanwhile, heat vegetable oil in small saucepan; deep-fry basil, in batches, until crisp.
4 Serve tomatoes sprinkled with basil.

serves 8

haloumi & spinach salad

13 prosciutto slices (200g)
500g asparagus, trimmed
200g haloumi cheese, sliced thinly
2 small pears (360g), cored, cut into thin wedges
200g baby spinach leaves
macadamia dressing
½ cup (75g) toasted macadamias, chopped coarsely
2 tablespoons sherry vinegar
¼ cup (60ml) macadamia oil

1 Preheat grill.
2 Cook prosciutto under preheated grill until crisp; break prosciutto into bite-size pieces.
3 Meanwhile, boil, steam or microwave asparagus until just tender; drain.
4 Make macadamia dressing.
5 Cook asparagus, cheese and pear on heated oiled grill plate (or grill or barbecue) until browned lightly.
6 Place prosciutto, asparagus, cheese, pear and spinach in large bowl with dressing; toss gently to combine.

macadamia dressing Place ingredients in screw-top jar; shake well.

serves 8
tip You can substitute olive oil for the macadamia oil, if you prefer.

roast chicken with lemon pistachio rice

1.4kg chicken
4 large potatoes
¼ cup (60ml) olive oil
2 teaspoons chopped fresh thyme
stuffing
¼ cup (60ml) olive oil
1 medium onion, chopped
⅓ cup (65g) long-grain rice
1 cup (250ml) chicken stock
1 cup (150g) pistachios
2 teaspoons chopped fresh thyme
2 teaspoons grated lemon rind

1 Make stuffing. Preheat oven to moderate.
2 Place stuffing in chicken, tie legs together, tuck wings under body. Place chicken, breast side up, in large baking dish. Bake in moderate oven 40 minutes.
3 Cut potatoes into 1cm slices. Place potato slices around chicken in dish. Drizzle chicken and potatoes with oil; sprinkle potatoes with thyme and pepper. Bake in moderate oven further 1 hour or until chicken is tender. Remove chicken from dish; keep warm.
4 Increase oven to very hot, bake potatoes further 15 minutes or until potatoes are browned and crisp. Serve roast chicken with potatoes.

stuffing Heat oil in saucepan, add onion; cook, stirring, until soft. Stir in rice until well coated. Stir in stock; simmer, covered, 20 minutes or until rice is tender and liquid has been absorbed. Remove from heat, stir in nuts, thyme and rind; cool.

serves 4

chicken with spinach & feta

¾ bunch (about 500g) spinach
75g feta cheese, crumbled
4 single chicken breast fillets
1 tablespoon olive oil
⅓ cup (80ml) double cream
2 tablespoons chopped fresh parsley
sauce
60g butter
2 tablespoons plain flour
1 cup (250ml) chicken stock
1 cup (250ml) dry white wine

1 Add washed spinach to saucepan; cook, stirring, until just wilted. Drain well; cool.
2 Combine spinach and cheese in bowl. Cut pocket in side of chicken, fill with spinach mixture; secure with toothpicks.
3 Heat oil in frying pan, add chicken; cook until browned both sides.
4 Make sauce. Pour over chicken; simmer, covered, 25 minutes. Stir in cream and parsley, stir until heated through.

sauce Melt butter in saucepan, add flour; stir over heat until bubbling. Remove from heat, gradually stir in stock and wine; stir over heat until sauce boils and thickens.

serves 4

creamy chicken filo pie

60g butter
4 bacon rashers, chopped
6 spring onions, chopped
2 cloves garlic, crushed
2 tablespoons plain flour
1½ cups (375ml) milk
3½ cups (525g) chopped cooked chicken
⅓ cup (25g) grated parmesan cheese
2 eggs, beaten lightly
10 sheets filo pastry
80g butter, melted, extra

1 Preheat oven to moderate. Lightly grease 23cm pie dish.
2 Heat butter in frying pan, add bacon, onions and garlic; cook, stirring, until bacon is crisp. Add flour; stir until combined. Remove from heat, gradually stir in milk. Return to heat and stir until mixture boils and thickens; cool. Stir in chicken, cheese and eggs.
3 To prevent pastry from drying out, cover with baking parchment then a damp tea towel until ready to use. Layer two sheets of pastry together, brushing each with a little extra butter. Fold layered sheets in half lengthways; place in prepared dish with edges overhanging. Repeat with another six pastry sheets and more extra butter, overlapping strips clockwise around dish until covered.
4 Spoon chicken mixture into dish, fold overhanging edges back onto filling; brush all over with more extra butter.
5 Layer remaining two pastry sheets with more extra butter; fold in half crossways, buttered sides together. Place pastry on top of pie, trim edge. Brush top lightly with more extra butter. Bake in moderate oven 35 minutes or until browned and heated through; cover with foil if pie begins to over-brown.

serves 6 to 8

greek meatballs in tomato sauce

800g minced beef
1 cup (70g) stale breadcrumbs
1 medium onion, chopped finely
2 cloves garlic, crushed
2 tablespoons chopped fresh thyme
2 tablespoons chopped fresh
  oregano
½ teaspoon ground cumin
1 egg, beaten lightly
2 tablespoons olive oil
2 tablespoons chopped fresh mint
tomato sauce
2 tablespoons olive oil
1 medium onion, chopped finely
2 cloves garlic, crushed
½ cup (125ml) dry red wine
2 x 425g cans tomatoes
⅓ cup (80ml) tomato paste
1 cup (250ml) chicken stock
2 tablespoons chopped fresh
  oregano
2 teaspoons sugar
pinch ground cinnamon

1 Combine mince, breadcrumbs, onion, garlic, thyme, oregano, cumin and egg in bowl, season with salt and pepper to taste; mix well. Roll 2 level tablespoons of mixture into a sausage-shaped meatball. Repeat with remaining mince mixture.
2 Heat oil in frying pan; cook meatballs, in batches, turning, until well browned. Drain on absorbent paper.
3 Make tomato sauce.
4 Add meatballs to tomato sauce; simmer, covered, 10 minutes or until cooked through. Sprinkle with chopped mint before serving.

tomato sauce Heat oil in saucepan, add onion and garlic; cook, stirring, until onion is soft. Add wine; simmer, uncovered, until reduced by half. Stir in undrained crushed tomatoes and remaining ingredients, season with salt and pepper to taste; simmer, uncovered, 10 minutes or until sauce is slightly thickened.

serves 4 to 6

beef with fennel

⅓ cup (80ml) olive oil
1 large onion, sliced
3 cloves garlic, sliced
1.25kg piece beef silverside
½ cup (125ml) dry red wine
2 cups (500ml) beef stock
6 sprigs fresh thyme
2 bay leaves
3 sprigs fresh oregano
1½ small fennel bulbs
2 tablespoons pine nuts, toasted
¼ cup chopped fresh parsley

1 Heat half the oil in frying pan, add onion and garlic; cook, stirring, until onion is soft; drain on absorbent paper. Sprinkle beef with salt and pepper to taste. Heat remaining oil in same pan, add beef; cook, turning, until browned all over.
2 Return onion mixture to pan, add combined wine and stock and herbs; cook, covered, over low heat 1½ hours, turning beef once during cooking.
3 Cut fennel into wedges, place in pan with beef; cook, covered, over low heat further 30 minutes or until beef and fennel are tender. Remove beef from pan, stand 10 minutes before serving.
4 Serve sliced beef with fennel and strained cooking liquid. Sprinkle with pine nuts and parsley.

serves 6

beef with aubergine & olives

1 large aubergine
coarse cooking salt
¼ cup (60ml) olive oil
1 tablespoon olive oil, extra
1kg diced beef steak
2 medium onions, chopped
2 teaspoons ground cumin
¼ teaspoon ground allspice
½ teaspoon ground cinnamon
½ teaspoon ground coriander
1 teaspoon paprika
¼ teaspoon cayenne pepper
4 cloves garlic, crushed
2 bay leaves
2 x 425g cans tomatoes
¼ cup (60ml) tomato paste
½ cup (125ml) water
1¾ cups (430ml) dry red wine
¼ cup (60ml) lemon juice
½ cup (90g) pitted black olives,
    quartered
½ cup (90g) pimiento-stuffed
    green olives, quartered
2 tablespoons chopped fresh
    flat-leaf parsley
½ teaspoon sugar

1 Cut aubergine into 2.5cm pieces, sprinkle with salt; stand 30 minutes. Rinse aubergine under cold water, drain; pat dry with absorbent paper.
2 Heat oil in large saucepan, add aubergine; cook until lightly browned. Remove aubergine from pan.
3 Heat extra oil in same pan, add beef in batches; cook until browned all over. Remove beef from pan.
4 Add onions to same pan; cook, stirring, until soft. Return beef to pan, add spices, garlic and bay leaves; cook, stirring, 1 minute.
5 Add undrained crushed tomatoes, paste, water and wine, stir until combined; simmer, covered, over low heat 1 hour, stirring occasionally. Add aubergine pieces; simmer, covered, 20 minutes or until aubergine and beef are tender. Add juice, olives, parsley and sugar; season with salt and pepper to taste, simmer until heated through.

serves 4 to 6

braised veal with pasta

1.7kg boned veal shoulder,
  rolled, tied
4 cloves garlic, sliced
¼ cup (60ml) olive oil
1 cinnamon stick
2 cloves
1 bay leaf
¼ cup (60ml) red wine vinegar

1 cup (250ml) dry red wine
2 tablespoons olive oil, extra
2 large onions, chopped
2 x 425g cans tomatoes
1 teaspoon sugar
pinch cayenne pepper
250g penne pasta
80g hard goats' cheese, grated

1 Preheat oven to low.

2 Rub veal with salt and pepper. With a sharp knife, make small incisions in veal; insert a slice of garlic in each incision, using half the garlic.

3 Heat oil in large flameproof dish, add veal; cook until browned all over. Add remaining garlic, cinnamon, cloves, bay leaf, vinegar and wine, bring to boil; cover tightly with foil and lid, bake in slow oven 1 hour, turning once.

4 Heat extra oil in saucepan, add onions; cook, stirring, until soft. Add undrained crushed tomatoes, sugar and cayenne; simmer, uncovered, 20 minutes or until thickened slightly.

5 Increase oven to moderately low. Add tomato mixture to veal in dish, cover; bake in moderately low oven 2 hours, turning veal occasionally. Remove veal from dish, keep warm. Skim fat from tomato mixture; discard cinnamon stick, cloves and bay leaf.

6 Cook pasta in pan of boiling water, uncovered, until tender; drain. Meanwhile, simmer tomato mixture 15 minutes or until thickened and reduced by half; season with salt and pepper to taste. You will need about 3½ cups (875ml) tomato sauce for this recipe. Slice veal.

7 Increase oven to moderately hot. Combine pasta, half the tomato sauce and half the cheese in bowl; spread over base of ovenproof dish (2 litre/8 cup capacity). Place veal on top of pasta, pour over remaining tomato sauce; sprinkle with remaining cheese. Bake, covered, in moderately hot oven 30 minutes or until heated through.

serves 6 to 8

roast pork with oranges & olives

2.5kg loin of pork, boned
1 tablespoon olive oil
1 tablespoon honey
1 tablespoon ouzo
1 tablespoon chopped fresh parsley
4 cloves garlic, crushed
1 cup (160g) pitted black olives
marinade
2 medium oranges
2 medium lemons
¾ cup (180ml) orange juice
¼ cup (60ml) lemon juice
1 tablespoon chopped fresh thyme
2 tablespoons honey
⅓ cup (80ml) ouzo

1 Place pork on bench, skin side up. Run knife 5mm under rind, gradually separating rind from pork. Trim excess fat; discard rind and fat. Roll pork firmly and secure with string at 2cm intervals.
2 Make marinade. Combine pork and marinade in large shallow dish, cover, refrigerate overnight; turn the pork occasionally.
3 Preheat oven to moderately hot.
4 Remove pork from marinade, reserve marinade. Combine oil, honey, ouzo, parsley and garlic in bowl, season with salt and pepper to taste; mix well. Place pork in baking dish. Brush honey mixture over pork. Bake, uncovered, in moderately hot oven 1 hour, brushing occasionally with the reserved marinade.
5 Add remaining reserved marinade and olives; bake, uncovered, further 10 minutes or until pork is tender. Remove pork and olives; stir pan juices over heat until slightly thickened. Remove string, serve pork with olives and pan juices.

marinade Using vegetable peeler, peel rind from oranges and lemons; cut rind into strips. Combine rind strips and remaining ingredients in bowl; mix well.

serves 6

pork & quince casserole

1 cup (220g) sugar
2 cups (500ml) water
2 small quince, quartered
⅓ cup (80ml) olive oil
1 large onion, sliced
2 cloves garlic, crushed
1kg diced pork
plain flour
1 cup (250ml) dry red wine
2 cups (500ml) beef stock
1 cinnamon stick
2 strips orange rind
2 tablespoons chopped fresh thyme

1 Combine sugar and water in saucepan; stir over heat, without boiling, until sugar is dissolved. Add quince; simmer, covered, 5 minutes or until just tender. Cool.
2 Heat half the oil in frying pan, add onion and garlic; cook, stirring, until onion is soft. Drain on absorbent paper.
3 Toss pork in flour, shake away excess flour. Heat remaining oil in same pan; cook pork, in batches, until lightly browned all over. Drain on absorbent paper.
4 Transfer onion mixture and pork to large saucepan, add combined wine, stock, cinnamon, rind and thyme; simmer, covered, 30 minutes, stirring occasionally.
5 Drain and chop quince; discard sugar syrup. Add quince to pork mixture, season with salt and pepper to taste; simmer, covered, further 30 minutes or until pork is tender.

serves 6

pork in garlic & walnut sauce

2 medium red peppers
2 tablespoons olive oil
4 medium pork loin chops
2 cloves garlic, crushed
410g can tomatoes
1 cinnamon stick
¾ cup (180ml) water
⅓ cup (80ml) dry white wine
garlic and walnut sauce
1 slice white bread
½ cup (60g) chopped walnuts
2 cloves garlic, crushed
¼ cup (60ml) white vinegar

1 Quarter peppers, remove seeds and membranes. Grill pepper pieces, skin side up, until skin blisters and blackens. Peel away skin, cut pepper into 2cm strips.
2 Heat oil in large saucepan; cook pork, in batches, until well browned. Remove from pan. Add garlic to pan with undrained crushed tomatoes, cinnamon, water and wine; bring to boil. Return pork to pan, add pepper; simmer, covered, 40 minutes or until pork is tender.
3 Make garlic and walnut sauce.
4 Take a little of the hot sauce from pan; stir into garlic and walnut sauce in bowl. Add garlic and walnut sauce to pan, season with salt and pepper to taste; stir until heated through. Discard cinnamon.

garlic and walnut sauce Cut crust from bread. Soak bread in cold water 2 minutes; drain, squeeze as much water as possible from bread. Process walnuts in food processor until finely chopped; remove to small bowl. Process bread, garlic and vinegar until smooth, add to walnuts in bowl; stir until well combined.

serves 4

lamb cabbage rolls

12 large cabbage leaves
1 tablespoon olive oil
1 medium onion, chopped
1 clove garlic, crushed
500g minced lamb
¼ cup (50g) long-grain rice
1 small tomato, peeled, chopped
1 tablespoon chopped fresh parsley
1 teaspoon chopped fresh dill
pinch ground cinnamon
2½ cups (625ml) hot chicken stock
20g butter
2 teaspoons cornflour
2 teaspoons water
1 egg, separated
2 tablespoons lemon juice

1 Add leaves, in batches, to large saucepan of boiling water, simmer, uncovered, until leaves are soft; drain, pat dry with absorbent paper. Cut any thick core from leaves.

2 Heat oil in saucepan, add onion and garlic; cook, stirring, until onion is soft. Cool. Combine mince, rice, tomato, herbs, cinnamon and onion mixture in bowl, season with salt and pepper to taste; mix well.

3 Divide mince mixture into 12 portions. Place a portion in centre of each cabbage leaf. Fold in sides of leaves and roll up to enclose filling. Place cabbage rolls close together over base of large pan. Pour over stock, dot with butter. Place a plate on top of the rolls to keep them in position during cooking; simmer, covered, over low heat 1 hour or until the rolls are cooked through.

4 Remove rolls from stock; keep warm. Simmer stock, uncovered, until reduced to ½ cup (125ml). Stir in blended cornflour and water; stir over heat until mixture boils and thickens slightly.

5 Beat egg white in small bowl of electric mixer until stiff peaks form; beat in egg yolk. Beat in juice and hot stock mixture. Return sauce to pan, whisk over heat until heated through; do not boil. Serve sauce with cabbage rolls.

makes 12

aubergine moussaka

2 large aubergines (about 1.2 kg)
coarse cooking salt
¼ cup (60ml) olive oil
2 tablespoons olive oil, extra
1 large onion, chopped
2 cloves garlic, crushed
1kg minced lamb
425g can tomatoes
2 tablespoons tomato paste
½ cup (125ml) dry red wine
2 tablespoons chopped fresh parsley

1 teaspoon sugar
¼ teaspoon ground cinnamon
¼ cup (20g) grated parmesan cheese
½ teaspoon ground nutmeg
cheese sauce
125g butter
⅔ cup (100g) plain flour
1 litre (4 cups) milk
½ cup (40g) grated parmesan cheese
2 eggs

1 Cut aubergines into 5mm slices, sprinkle with salt; stand 20 minutes.
Rinse aubergine under cold water; drain, pat dry with absorbent paper.
Place aubergine slices in single layer on lightly greased oven trays. Brush
with oil, grill on both sides until lightly browned; drain on absorbent paper.
2 Heat extra oil in pan, add onion and garlic; cook, stirring, until onion is soft.
Add mince; cook, stirring, until mince is browned. Add undrained crushed
tomatoes, paste, wine, parsley, sugar and cinnamon, season with salt and
pepper to taste; simmer, covered, 30 minutes.
3 Preheat oven to moderate. Grease ovenproof dish (2.5 litre/10 cup capacity).
4 Make cheese sauce.
5 Line prepared dish with one-third of the aubergine, top with half the meat
sauce, then half the remaining aubergine, remaining meat sauce and remaining
aubergine.
6 Spread cheese sauce over aubergine, sprinkle with cheese and nutmeg.
Bake, uncovered, in moderate oven 45 minutes or until lightly browned.

cheese sauce Melt butter in saucepan, stir in flour; continue stirring over
heat until bubbling. Remove from heat, gradually stir in milk; stir over heat until
mixture boils and thickens. Remove from heat, stir in cheese, cool slightly;
stir in eggs, mix until smooth.

serves 6

roast garlic lamb with lemon potatoes

½ cup (125ml) olive oil
2 tablespoons grated lemon rind
2 tablespoons lemon juice
2 tablespoons dry white wine
2 teaspoons seasoned pepper
2 tablespoons chopped fresh thyme
2kg leg of lamb
2 cloves garlic, sliced
1 tablespoon fresh rosemary leaves
lemon potatoes
12 medium old potatoes
¼ cup (60ml) olive oil
⅓ cup (80ml) lemon juice
1½ tablespoons grated lemon rind
2 tablespoons chopped fresh
   rosemary
2 tablespoons chopped fresh thyme
1½ teaspoons cracked black
   peppercorns

1 Combine oil, rind, juice, wine, pepper and thyme in jug; mix well. Trim excess fat from lamb. Using point of knife, make 12 incisions evenly over top of lamb leg. Place a slice of garlic and some of the rosemary leaves in each incision. Pour oil mixture over lamb; cover, refrigerate 3 hours or overnight, turning occasionally.
2 Preheat oven to moderately hot.
3 Drain lamb, reserve marinade. Place lamb in large baking dish; bake, uncovered, in moderately hot oven 40 minutes.
4 Make lemon potatoes; add to lamb. Bake, turning occasionally, further 50 minutes, or until lamb and potatoes are tender.
5 Remove lamb from baking dish, cover, keep warm. Drain juices from pan; reserve juices.
6 Increase oven to very hot. Return potatoes to oven, bake further 20 minutes or until potatoes are browned and crisp. Heat reserved marinade and reserved juices in pan, bring to boil. Serve with sliced lamb and lemon potatoes.

lemon potatoes Cut potatoes into 3cm pieces, place in bowl. Pour over combined remaining ingredients and salt; mix well.

serves 6

pastitso

250g macaroni
2 eggs, beaten lightly
¾ cup (60g) grated parmesan
   cheese
2 tablespoons stale breadcrumbs
meat sauce
2 tablespoons olive oil
2 medium onions, chopped
750g minced lamb (or beef)
425g can tomatoes
⅓ cup (80ml) tomato paste
½ cup (125ml) water
¼ cup (60ml) dry white wine
1 teaspoon beef stock powder
½ teaspoon ground cinnamon
1 egg, beaten lightly
topping
90g butter
½ cup (75g) plain flour
3½ cups (875ml) milk
1 cup (80g) grated parmesan
   cheese
2 egg yolks

1 Preheat oven to moderate. Grease shallow ovenproof dish (2.5 litre/10 cup capacity).

2 Make meat sauce.

3 Meanwhile, add pasta to large pan of boiling water, boil, uncovered, until just tender; drain. Combine hot pasta, eggs and cheese in bowl; mix well.

4 Meanwhile, make topping.

5 Press pasta over base of prepared dish. Top pasta evenly with meat sauce, pour over topping, smooth surface; sprinkle with breadcrumbs. Bake, uncovered, in moderate oven 1 hour or until lightly browned. Stand 10 minutes before serving.

meat sauce Heat oil in pan, add onions and mince; cook, stirring, until mince is well browned. Stir in undrained crushed tomatoes, paste, water, wine, stock powder and cinnamon; simmer, uncovered, until thick. Cool. Stir in egg.

topping Melt butter in pan, add flour; stir over heat until bubbling, remove from heat, gradually stir in milk. Stir over heat until sauce boils and thickens, stir in cheese; cool slightly. Stir in egg yolks.

serves 6 to 8

marinated tuna kebabs

1kg piece of fresh tuna
marinade
½ cup fresh parsley sprigs
½ cup fresh coriander leaves
3 cloves garlic, bruised
1 teaspoon ground cinnamon
1 teaspoon ground cumin
1 teaspoon ground sweet paprika
1 teaspoon ground coriander
½ cup (125ml) lemon juice
¼ cup (60ml) olive oil
1 teaspoon grated lemon rind

1 Cut tuna into 3cm cubes.
2 Blend or process all ingredients for marinade until smooth.
3 Combine tuna and marinade in large bowl, mix well; cover, refrigerate overnight.
4 Thread tuna onto 8 skewers, grill or barbecue until cooked as desired, turning once during cooking. Serve with lemon wedges, if desired.

makes 8
tip Soak bamboo skewers in water for several hours or overnight to prevent them from burning.

baked lemon & tomato sardines

8 large fresh sardines (about 400g)
3 medium tomatoes, sliced
⅓ cup (80ml) olive oil
2 tablespoons grated lemon rind

2½ tablespoons lemon juice
2 cloves garlic, crushed
2 tablespoons chopped fresh parsley
1 tablespoon chopped fresh oregano

1 Preheat oven to moderately hot.
2 Cut heads from sardines and remove entrails. Cut through underside of sardines to backbone; rinse under cold water.
3 Cut backbone through at tail end with scissors without piercing skin. Pull backbone out towards head end to remove. Remove small bones, press sardines flat.
4 Place tomato slices in single layer in two 20cm x 30cm baking tins. Place sardines, skin side up, over tomatoes, pour over combined oil, rind, juice and garlic; sprinkle with herbs. Bake, uncovered, in moderately hot oven 7 minutes or until cooked through.

serves 4

baked cod fishcakes with garlic sauce

500g dried salt cod
4 medium potatoes
1 small onion, grated
1 egg, beaten lightly
2 tablespoons milk
2 tablespoons chopped fresh flat-leaf
  parsley
½ teaspoon ground black pepper
2 tablespoons olive oil

garlic sauce
10 slices (250g) stale white bread
5 cloves garlic, crushed
¼ cup (60ml) olive oil
2 tablespoons lemon juice
1 tablespoon water
2 tablespoons ground almonds

1 Place cod in bowl, cover well with cold water, cover; stand overnight.
2 Drain cod, place in saucepan, cover with cold water; simmer, uncovered, 15 minutes. Drain, pat dry with absorbent paper. Flake cod finely, remove any skin and bones.
3 Meanwhile, boil, steam or microwave potatoes until tender; mash well.
4 Preheat oven to moderately hot. Lightly grease oven tray.
5 Combine cod, potatoes, onion, egg, milk, parsley and pepper in bowl. With wet hands, roll ⅓ cup mixture into a ball; flatten slightly. Repeat with remaining mixture.
6 Place patties on prepared tray, brush patties with oil; bake in moderately hot oven 10 minutes. Turn patties over, reduce heat to moderate, bake further 20 minutes or until lightly browned.
7 Meanwhile, make garlic sauce. Serve codfish patties with garlic sauce.

garlic sauce Trim crusts from bread. Soak bread in cold water 2 minutes. Drain, squeeze as much water as possible from bread. Combine bread and remaining ingredients with salt and pepper to taste in bowl; mix well.

makes 12

fish fillets with tomato herb crust

¼ cup (60ml) olive oil

1 clove garlic, crushed

2 medium onions, sliced

2 trimmed celery stalks (200g),
   chopped

3 medium tomatoes, peeled,
   chopped

¾ cup chopped fresh parsley

4 fish fillets (use a firm white fish,
   such as cod, hake or whiting)

1 teaspoon dried oregano leaves

1 medium lemon, sliced thinly

½ cup (125ml) dry white wine

¼ cup (60ml) lemon juice

¼ cup (15g) stale breadcrumbs

1 Preheat oven to moderate.

2 Heat oil in frying pan, add garlic, onions and celery; cook, stirring, until onions are soft. Add tomatoes, cook, stirring, until tomatoes are soft; add parsley, mix well.

3 Place fish in single layer in baking dish, sprinkle with oregano; season with salt and pepper. Top with tomato mixture.

4 Layer lemon slices over tomato mixture, pour over combined wine and juice, sprinkle with breadcrumbs. Bake, uncovered, in moderate oven 30 minutes or until fish is tender.

serves 4

octopus in red wine

2kg baby octopus
⅓ cup (80ml) olive oil
2 cloves garlic, crushed
500g baby onions, quartered
2 bay leaves
1½ cups (375ml) dry red wine
1 cup (250ml) water
¼ cup (60ml) red wine vinegar
440ml can tomato purée
1 teaspoon chicken stock powder
2 teaspoons dried oregano leaves
2 teaspoons sugar
1 tablespoon chopped fresh parsley

1 Cut heads from octopus just below eyes, discard heads; remove beaks. Wash octopus; cut into quarters.
2 Heat oil in saucepan, add octopus and garlic; cook, stirring, until most of the octopus liquid is evaporated.
3 Add onions, bay leaves, wine, water, vinegar, purée and stock powder. Simmer, uncovered, 1½ hours or until octopus are tender, stirring occasionally. Remove bay leaves, add oregano and sugar, season with salt and pepper to taste; mix well. Sprinkle with parsley just before serving.

serves 4

glossary

allspice also known as pimento or jamaican pepper; available whole or ground.

almonds, ground also known as almond meal, we used packaged commercially ground nuts.

artichoke hearts tender centre of the globe artichoke; purchased in brine canned or in jars.

aubergine also known as eggplant. Depending on their age, they may need to be sliced and salted to reduce their bitterness. Rinse and dry well before use.

beans

broad also known as fava, windsor or horse beans; they are available dried, fresh, canned and frozen. Fresh and frozen, they are best peeled twice (discarding both the outer long green pod and beige-green tough inner shell).

haricot small, white, oval beans with a smooth texture and bland in flavour. Require soaking.

cayenne pepper thin-fleshed, long, very-hot red chilli; usually purchased dried and ground.

cheese

feta a crumbly textured goat's- or sheep's-milk cheese with a sharp, salty taste.

goats' cheese made from goats' milk, it has an earthy, strong taste. Can be purchased in both soft and firm textures, in various shapes and sizes, sometimes rolled in ash or herbs.

graviera hard sheeps' milk cheese with a mild taste. Gruyere can be used as a substitute.

haloumi a firm, cream-coloured sheep's milk cheese originating in Cyprus. Matured in brine, it can be grilled or fried, briefly, without breaking down.

parmesan a sharp-tasting, dry, hard cheese, made from skimmed or semi-skimmed milk and aged for at least a year.

chillies available in many different types and sizes. Use rubber gloves when chopping fresh chillies as they can burn your skin.

chives related to the onion and leek, with subtle onion flavour.

cinnamon stick dried inner bark of the shoots of the cinnamon tree.

coriander also known as cilantro and Chinese parsley. A strongly flavoured herb, use it sparingly. Available fresh, ground and in seed form.

cornflour also known as cornstarch; used as a thickening agent in cooking.

courgettes also known as zucchini.

cumin available both ground and as whole seeds; cumin has a warm, earthy, rather strong flavour.

fennel bulb vegetable, also known as finocchio or anise. Also the name given to dried seeds having a licorice flavour.

fennel seeds dried seeds having a licorice flavour.

filo pastry chilled or frozen tissue-thin pastry sheets that are very versatile, lending themselves to both sweet and savoury dishes.

flat-leaf parsley also known as continental parsley or italian parsley.

herbs we have specified when to use fresh or dried herbs. Use dried (not ground) herbs in the proportions of 1:4 for fresh herbs, for example 1 teaspoon dried herbs instead of 4 teaspoons (1 tablespoon) chopped fresh herbs.

lemon pepper seasoning a blend of black pepper, lemon, herbs and spices.

lemon thyme a variety of thyme with a lemony fragrance.

macadamias native to Australia, a rich and buttery nut; store in refrigerator due to its high oil content.

olive oil mono-unsaturated oil; made from pressing tree-ripened olives. Extra virgin and virgin are the best, obtained from the first pressings of the olive, while extra light or light refers to the taste, not fat levels.

ouzo aniseed-flavoured Greek spirit.

paprika ground dried red bell pepper (capsicum); available sweet or hot.

peppercorns available in black, white, red or green.

pine nuts also known as pignoli; small, cream-coloured kernels obtained from the cones of different varieties of pine trees.

pistachios pale green, delicately flavoured nut inside hard off-white shells. To peel, soak shelled nuts in boiling water about 5 minutes; drain, then pat dry.

prosciutto salted-cured, air-dried (unsmoked), pressed ham; usually sold in paper-thin slices, ready to eat.

quince yellow-skinned fruit with hard texture and acid taste.

salt cod dried salted cod; also called baccala.

tomato paste tomato puree used to flavour soups, stews, sauces and casseroles.

vine leaves we used vine leaves in brine; they are available in jars and packets.

vinegar

balsamic authentic only from the province of Modena, Italy; made from a regional wine of white trebbiano grapes specially processed then aged in antique wooden casks to give the exquisite pungent flavour.

red wine based on fermented red wine.

sherry mellow wine vinegar named for its colour.

white made from spirit of cane sugar.

conversion charts

MEASURES

The cup and spoon measurements used in this book are metric: one measuring cup holds approximately 250ml; one metric tablespoon holds 20ml; one metric teaspoon holds 5ml.

All cup and spoon measurements are level.

The most accurate way of measuring dry ingredients is to weigh them. When measuring liquids, use a clear glass or plastic jug with metric markings.

We use large eggs with an average weight of 60g.

warning This book may contain recipes for dishes made with raw or lightly cooked eggs. These should be avoided by vulnerable people such as pregnant and nursing mothers, invalids, the elderly, babies and young children.

DRY MEASURES

METRIC	IMPERIAL
15g	½oz
30g	1oz
60g	2oz
90g	3oz
125g	4oz (¼lb)
155g	5oz
185g	6oz
220g	7oz
250g	8oz (½lb)
280g	9oz
315g	10oz
345g	11oz
375g	12oz (¾lb)
410g	13oz
440g	14oz
470g	15oz
500g	16oz (1lb)
750g	24oz (1½lb)
1kg	32oz (2lb)

LIQUID MEASURES

METRIC	IMPERIAL
30ml	1 fl oz
60ml	2 fl oz
100ml	3 fl oz
125ml	4 fl oz
150ml	5 fl oz (¼ pint/1 gill)
190ml	6 fl oz
250ml	8 fl oz
300ml	10 fl oz (½ pint)
500ml	16 fl oz
600ml	20 fl oz (1 pint)
1000ml (1 litre)	1¾ pints

LENGTH MEASURES

METRIC	IMPERIAL
3mm	⅛in
6mm	¼in
1cm	½in
2cm	¾in
2.5cm	1in
5cm	2in
6cm	2½in
8cm	3in
10cm	4in
13cm	5in
15cm	6in
18cm	7in
20cm	8in
23cm	9in
25cm	10in
28cm	11in
30cm	12in (1ft)

OVEN TEMPERATURES

These oven temperatures are only a guide for conventional ovens.
For fan-assisted ovens, check the manufacturer's manual.

	°C (CELSIUS)	°F (FAHRENHEIT)	GAS MARK
Very low	120	250	½
Low	150	275–300	1–2
Moderately low	160	325	3
Moderate	180	350–375	4–5
Moderately hot	200	400	6
Hot	220	425–450	7–8
Very hot	240	475	9

index